MORE AMOR

More Amor

Valentine Verses

Jafet Reyes-Cisneros

For Primavera

Acknowledgements

I wish to thank God, Jesus the Light Being, for the inspiration to write these poems. Every poem began in my sleep as words and lines that coalesced. I would keep them in my memory until I awoke and then immediately recorded them. As I would write the rest of the poems afterward, I felt His finger pointing the way.

Throughout the years, I have grown fully aware that His divine hand has always guided me and will continue to do so until the end of my earthly days. Souls are light, and my light shines bright. My body will decay, but my soul will join Him in eternity. Glory to the Highest for He has allowed me to give birth to mirth—my children, my poems.

I also deeply thank my family for their unwavering support. Thank you for reading my poems as I composed them and for giving me invaluable feedback. Thank you for being my first fans.

Message to the Reader

Dear reader,

    As I read to publish my previous book, "Beneath the Shadow of the Almond Tree", I realized that the majority of my poems were melancholic and saddening. They were lamentations, reflective of the dark days that I had experienced throughout life. Though, at times, it helps us to find words that echo with our suffering souls, I sought to find hope, spread love, and inspire hearts and minds with my new book, "More Amor".

    After writing my first book, I took the time to heal and prepare for my second. I was a broken man before, but now I am born anew. It is my sincerest hope that you find solace, cheer, and happiness when you read my poems. Though a few are tragic, most of this book's poems exude a newfound optimism—a replenished faith –that I hope to share and, if you allow me, plant like a seed within you, so that it may sprout when you interact with others and face the adversities of life.

Let these words serve as mana of hope to the present and future generations so that humanity does not forget to smile, laugh, kiss, but, foremost—believe: believe that tomorrow's sun will be brighter, believe that love, justice, mercy, and all good things are still present on this Earth, believe in God and that the Light Being works all of life's aspects in our favor and for our benefit.

Content

"More Amor"

Her name was Consuela, and she had fled Venezuela
Rocking in her chair, she'd share the proverbs of Abuela[1]
Her English was seasoned with the Spanish of many seasons
As she'd remind me that I was, to live, one of her reasons

Her words—a *sancocho*[2] of Spanglish— lacked finesse
Though of tenderness and kindness, she was the patroness
Her sun-seen skin was made, not of brass, but topaz
Every syllable salsa dancing with the pizzazz of jazz!

Her womb, a sinfree spring of motherly mirth
Pietà animated to life by the breath of my birth
Jeanne d'Arc fearlessly fighting for family against the dark
The dark sharks that hunt her as if her accent were a mark

---

[1] *Abuela* is Spanish for "grandmother". Pronounced "ah-BOO-eh-lah".
[2] *Sancocho* is a type of Latin American broth whose ingredients vary greatly depending on the country and culture that prepares it. However, it always consists of a large mixture of ingredients.

Society had forced on her

      the scarlet mask of the immigrant

In a rabid, contemptuous attempt to conceal

      that which made her magnificent

Had they tried, they would had pushed prejudice aside

      and seen the face of Mary inside

And that the mask had— not with shame—but rather

      with pride and blood, been dyed

Thus, I leave you with the proverb

      that adorns the door of her store

Pain is like an ocean,

      and we, a seashore

So do not roar with rage

      against those that are sore

For what every eroded soul,

      all of us, need is more *amor*[3]

---

[3] *Amor* is Spanish for "love". Pronounced "ah-MORE".

"The Staircase of Memory"

In my mind,

    Night is day,

        And each day

            Is in May.

            And my soul

      Sings King Cole[4]

    It is whole

And it's gold.

Like a charm,

    Held her arm

        It is warm

            There's no harm.

            But alas,

      I come last,

    And the past

Has long passed.

---

[4] Nat King Cole was a famous pianist and singer of jazz in the 1940s and 1950s.

"The Riddle of the Elf Lord"

Henceforth here, I, the Elf Lord of Richport[5]

Pass on a riddle of utmost import

It's a thing sought by all sort

Some, seriously; some, for sport

A game where two can play and both win

A blessed quest for that which is within

That which humanity eternally seeks to begin

Though, once lost, 'tis titanic to return where it has been

A thing best expressed through acts and not words

Where a pair is best and, too much, a third

The song sang along by spring songbirds

Which delights its audience's ears when heard

---

[5] *Puerto Rico* is Spanish for "Rich Port".

Without it, life is a tree with no leaves
Precious, though, it can't be stolen by thieves
Mana of hope to he who, in it, believes
Summer showers to the flower that receives

None must pay back this exponential debt
For none, enough of this, may give or get
The brave and the bold pursue this gamble, this bet
Heaven's voices twining and rhyming in duet

Unmeasurable by the wisest in the land
The reason why frozen is the clock's hour hand
Heartache to heartache, resilient, it still stands
Crosses continents and can't be buried by sand

The timeless play playing in the Theatre of Time
A basket brimming with grape and lime
Youth's flame yet elders' thyme
The reason for the romantic's rhyme

Thus, I, the Elf Lord of Richport, speak
From creek to peak, the answer to this one riddle, seek
For I must return to dancing with her, cheek to cheek
As, through us, pass the years, months, and weeks.

"Rain Rises"

Rain rises in the graveyard boulevard where my heart is scarred

Her hair between my fingers as we hide behind her yard

Mine is the girl of the amber curls, the twirling gardens

That I still see as the curtains close and the bedroom darkens.

Snow rises in the day of Noel

Her hips held by my hands as I kiss Belle

Smiling, she casts, on me, a spell

What the future holds, I cannot yet tell.

Sunset on the east, sunrise from the west

As I awaken with a merry fairy asleep on my chest

I have asked Time to not pass,

But, many times, time does not last.

What falls from the sky rises from the earth

It is all a cycle of death and birth

Thus, I await the next lifetime for us to meet

As two strangers sharing an umbrella in the street.

In this first versed morning memory, my mind everlastingly lingers

Regardless of countless centuries, my heart rests in her lily fingers

Two lovers, never apart

Our story, from end to start.

MORE AMOR

"Beatrice Bee"

Beatrice Bee was my La La Land
I, her Sheik of Araby
But, alas, I chose the grand jazz band
Over sweet Beatrice Bee

Now, stuck I am
    amidst this Sahara sand
This introverted desert that stretches
    from me to the sea
I can barely stand, my emotions are a storm of sand,
    I can't see my hand
But I trudge onward,
    guiding me the North Star that is Beatrice Bee

Like desert days, days with
    her were hot and cold
Though, instead, cool was the noon
    and warm was the moon
Oh, what a bedside sight, what a morning melody
    was Beatrice Bee to behold
Oh, worry not, heart—sleep, heart—amidst the dunes,
    for I promise you will see her soon

I still taste the *sabor*[6] of her *color*[7]
Sea salt mined with the nip of my lip
I still feel the *sudor*[8] of her *ardor*[9]
My grip on her hip, rudder of her ship

Ay, *amor*[10], my *dolor*[11] is a welded door
Keeping my feelings trapped like pyramids of yore
Keeping my feelings buried like unrefined ore
Keeping my feelings stranded like a shipwrecked ship in a shore

---

[6] *Sabor* is Spanish for "taste". Pronounced "sah-BORE".
[7] *Color* is Spanish for "color". Pronounced "co-LORE".
[8] *Sudor* is Spanish for "sweat". Pronounced "sue-DORE".
[9] *Ardor* is Spanish for "ardor", "heat", "zeal". Pronounced "are-DORE".
[10] *Amor* is Spanish for "love". In context, here it is used as "beloved". Pronounced "ah-MORE".
[11] *Dolor* is Spanish for "pain". Pronounced "doe-LORE".

The arena of *arena*[12]

    plays *el desierto*'s[13] concerto

Whistling winds

    carrying my *lamento*[14]

Gone is my afternoon sun,

    then my ruby, my beauty, my burgundy belle

I fear I hear bells' knell[15],

    so let the seaside, sealike sands of the Sahara spell

I am the Sheik of Araby

This is who I am, this is who I be

The long-lost lover of Beatrice Bee.

---

[12] *Arena* is Spanish for "sand". Pronounced "ah-REH-nah".

[13] *El desierto* is Spanish for "the desert". Pronounced "EL day-SEE-ERR-toh".

[14] *Lamento* is Spanish for "lamentation". Pronounced "lah-MEN-toh".

[15] Knell is the sound that bells make when slowly rung, as if in a somber event like in a funeral.

"Cats and Dogs"

Cats and dogs are no fun

When cats and dogs don't get along

Cats and dogs fight over the Sun

Cats and dogs, sing a song!

Cats and dogs, everywhere!

Over there and in my hair!

In her dress and in Congress

Making sure we have less!

Cats and dogs will burn this town

Cat-dogs even bit the downcast clown

Cats and dogs dislike wise words

Mad cats, bad dogs—nothing but a herd

Bark! Meow!

The cacophony of the stirred
Making sure reason is unheard
Cats and dogs dislike any more than a third
No room for tweets, not even if you're a bird!

How absurd!

Cats and dogs have their charm
But their bites cause much harm
Ripping your flesh from self as they conquer this Animal Farm
Whipping the birds and horses as flesh eating mosquitoes swarm.

Cats and dogs, each other's rear, will sniff

Putrid poop, they love to take a whiff

No need for paper when you're a cat

You simply lick it and that's that!

Beware, my people, cats and dogs!

Like slithering snakes, they begird[16]

Till they hear us bark the absurd,

Meow and bow for squealing hogs,

And still lies Lee's mute mockingbird!

---

[16] To begird is "to encircle, to surround".

"The World Will End in Song"

Some say the world will end in fire

Others say the world will end in ice

Some whisper it shall end in ire

Others utter that it shall end in vice

Dark have been my dreams of late

As I wait to see the world's twilight fate

Armageddon! Ragnarök! I anticipate

As nightly terrors and deprivations accumulate

"Have you heard the good news?" Peter penned

For Peter knew how the world would end

Peter knew from a friend that again

A friend from heaven's throne, God will send!

Men and women don't know— this story long before was penned
Men and women are wrong: the world will not end long
And now this poet pens: in none of these, the world will end
"Worry not," speaks your Friend, "the world will end in song."

In the end, we will spend, much time, forgiving and making amends
Eternity, for our souls to mend, we will have as godsend
Before to streets of gold and seas of sapphire, our souls ascend
Before to heavenly light and sacred fire, our souls transcend

The heavenly will sing hymns
The chorus will sing to Him
The Light Being will never dim
And with joy, my soul will brim!

The fate of the faithful is full of bliss

So remember when the world is amiss

Remember when your heart, mind and spirit sags with melancholy

When hopeless you feel at witnessing humanity's folly

When war and famine is all you hear

When your eyes cannot stop dripping tears

When you feel lost and without a place to belong

When everything in this reality seems wrong

The world. Will end. In song.

"Throw Away This Paper if Not Read by September"

Dear Klein,[17]

If you read this paper note on time,
Know that forever you will be mine
Never will we sever our souls, twined,
And always, for you, I will write rhyme.

However, if you do not read this letter by September,
Know that our velvet covered summer did not last forever,
And summer love did not make me any more, any lesser.

But if I never see you again, my skin will remember
Midsummer kisses in the eternal winter of Denver.

To waking up, wrapped and warm in your arms, beloved,

– Amber

---

[17] Klein is pronounced "Kline", rhyming with the word "mine".

"Strolling Down the Park with My Red Balloon"

She is my red balloon
And I, her would-be groom
Spending with her in June
A yellow afternoon

Strolling down the park, the happiest sight is you floating up
Just a string connects us two, but a string is more than enough

My little, red airhead, let me blow air inside of you
So that, up and up, you'll float for both—float for us two

Rise beyond the green grass and tall trees toward the sky
But then I'll tug you back to me so that you'll float by my side

So full of joy, she fills up the room
A little more, and she would go "BOOM"!

Every red balloon needs a counterweight
A guardian to make sure she doesn't deviate
Lest he lets go and, oh, the poor balloon is lost
To fickle wind's mighty blows and harpy feather gusts

Together, dear, let's spend this sunny weather afternoon
Don't worry, dear, I'll never let go of you, my little, red balloon

MORE AMOR

"Haiku of the Blue Bamboos"

See the blue bamboos

Pandas painted blue by moons

Singing hues of blues

"Parenthood"

Small balls of snow drop
To the highest mountain top
Little trinkets of rain make
Full the deepest lake.

So do your little kisses land
On these silver hair strands
For tiny love sincerities
Fill this still beating heart with serenity.

"There"

Forehead to forehead, we were there
Underneath the debonair[18] stair

For her, just, for her, this affair
A flare that threatens to burn this pair

But I burn for her like a blue flame
For her red hair and her slender frame

When we're together, we go back to the same
A never ending game of claim and shame

So she asks, "We meet where?"
In the stair where we were

All is well when we're there
My fingers[19] through your hair

---

[18] Debonair means "suave, sophisticated, charming, especially of a man".
[19] Meant to be read as "fin-GERS".

I'll keep you warm amidst this snow
In the place that us lovers know

Be my beau[20] and set me aglow
My ember that, with each kiss, grows

Plunge your tongue without pause
Bite my lips just because

Give in to love that must
Rekindle all that was

Let you and I be us
In you, again, get lost

Your warmth, my heart, defrost
And to the past, we cross

[20] Beau means "male lover". Pronounced "BOW", rhyming with the word "low".

MORE AMOR

"Hungry No More"

Not more than a lifetime ago,

There lived a woman and her child

In a cottage buried in snow

And surrounded by mountain wild.

She named her sable[21] haired son Lycanphil[22]

And raised her boy away from those who smear[23]

For his icy stare brought many a chill

And all, but his own, fell or ran in fear.

The poor boy was as hairy as a bear

And, by age twelve, had a full, lycan[24] beard

Only his mother gave him tender care

For the rest only considered him weird.

---

[21] Sable means "dark; black".

[22] Lycanphil is pronounced "LIE-can-fill".

[23] Smear means "to vilify; to try to destroy the reputation of".

[24] A lycan is a human who can willingly transform into a werewolf and back to its human form.

Lycanphil lived for the hunt and thrill
Of piercing rosy flesh with knife and teeth
He killed with a ravening[25] wolf's skill
And slurped the red wine off the hunted meat.

No matter the weight and height of prey,
Regardless of the many meats he tried,
Hunger would soon again creep and stay—
The emptiness inside would not subside.

Starved and shunned, he searched for finer meat,
A chicken, a fish, a horse, and a goat.
His teeth ripped all life he could eat
As spleens, livers, and hearts descended his throat.

---

[25] Ravening means "devouring with greed and desire".

One day, his lycan eyes fell on the mill

As his stomach growled like roaring thunder.

With stealth, Lycanphil went in for the kill

To satiate his animal hunger.

His sight fixed on a man in a clearing,

Timing his attack with the turn of the blades.

Their eyes meeting, the man felt a shearing[26],

A shearing of flesh that he wished to degrade.

Wolf fangs carved and ripped into the man's waist,

Tearing a chunk of skin, muscle, and bone.

Lycanphil was briefly filled by his taste

Yet, after, he had never felt so alone.

---

[26] Shearing means "the act of cutting using two parallel, opposite forces, as if with scissors."

Bloodstained and tainted, the boy sprinted home
To the cottage buried in mountain snow
But the home was empty—and on, he roamed
Searching for the warmth of winters ago.

Thus, thirteen thousand moons arose and fell.
The lycan's legend, like wildfire, grew,
But, we have yet to reach Antarctic hell
In this campfire tale for guests like you.

One sunny but chilly morning of June,
A maiden went into the deepest wood
Searching for green gods' gifts 'til the full moon
Slowly ascended atop her red hood.

Lycanphil howled and prowled about his prey,
Inhaling the aroma of fresh flesh,
But when Red Hood saw him, she sat to play
And stretched her hand to pat and enmesh[27].

The beast egressed[28]—his belly, the sorest—
As he cautiously exited the wood.
Her fingers ingressed[29] his furry forest
As he whiffed and licked, with restraint, Red Hood

So, he whisked her away, as their lips locked,
To the cottage buried in mountain snow
And, for an instance, so stop did the clock,
Each kiss rekindling warmth from long ago.

---

[27] Enmesh means "to entangle as if using a system of cords, wires, or threads."
[28] Egress means "to exit; to emerge". Pronounced "E-gress".
[29] Ingress means "to enter". Pronounced "IN-gress".

Only then, with each caress,
His heart hurt less and less
No longer was his soul sore
He felt hunger no more

Look yonder, beyond the treescape and snow
And you'll see a faint lamp aglow
In the cottage, he's found his mate of old
But where is yours, oh, lonely soul?

Listen! From frigid hell, the lycan howls in the dead of night,
And the true victim of this tragedy now makes their debut.
Awaken, stand up and go outside—look up, down, left and right,
For the victims are all those who hunger—they, I, and you.

MORE AMOR

"Marry Me, Kimberly"

Marry me, Kimberly
Be my nymph's symphony
That I play day and night
Outside and out of sight

Marry me, Kimberly
You are all I can see.
In the sky, like a kite
Reflecting the sunlight

Marry me, Kimberly
Give me your company
Be every day's delight
My home's hearth now ignite.

What is a house without cheerful children and wife?
What is a bed unless there's someone to share with for life?

Become my bride, beloved, my magical, white sprite
Who flies me away to astounding, heavenly heights
Up and up, we say, until we see the sky so bright!

Have a bouquet of roses and find, hidden, a rosy heart inside
Agree to a lifetime of adventures as my treasured bride

Simply say "I do"
And I'll be yours too!
I swear to be true
And hue the days blue!

Take my hand and let's dance
Swinging beneath the streetscape of streetlights
And end the night with the chance
That you will be my tomorrow's first sight

Let our names, with a lovely reverie[30], be a synonym
Be my angel, Kim, and, with me, create cheerful cherubim

A ring fashioned, from a blade of grass, signaled our matrimony
A choir of your plushies attended the ceremony

A pink dress, a jeans jacket, and a pair of black boots, she wore
Before this luminous angel, what more can I ask for?

---

[30] A reverie is a daydream—a state of absent-minded musing.

Every moment in your presence is a present

Your nightly kisses, in my presence, leave your scent

Pressing my lip against your hip, I ascent

And whisper verses in your ear with a Latin accent.

Even after we are married, I will ask you to marry!

Let each moon be a honeymoon as, in your skin, I pour honey

Kiss me and touch me—marry me, Kimberly

Make each day, a daydream, and each song, a symphony!

MORE AMOR

"Jack the Jester"

There was once a king so fond of cats

That, instead of a crown, he wore a hat

And atop this hat sat the Queen of Cats

Who invited Jack the Jester for a chat.

The queen meowed and purred for her guest

As the jester introduced himself with a jest:

"Oh, pretty pussy, the most beautiful in all the land,

Long I have studied feline anatomy with my hands,

Though I am mere jester, I am a master of CAT scans,

And from many magical courts, jealous kings have had me banned.

See, the name given to me by my mother is John Richard

Odd, but much mistrust caused my name in the court of a wizard

So allow me to delight you until the day of Saint Nick

And please forgo my legal name and instead call me Dick.

I'm always abreast with all the most titillating topics
Elections, soccer, black holes, and architecture most Gothic
I can tell you tales of travels to locations most tropic
Or the rising Gotham skyscrapers that defy all logic.

I am the master jester, voyager of myriad ports
Apt explorer of all lands and all pussies of all sorts
Conquered, I have, with comely comedy, the fiercest forts
So, pray, please allow me to entertain you and your court."

All the palace pussies,
        to the king belonged
Oh, but little did the king know,
        every pussy, for the master jester, longed
If it were up to the king,
        he would let them go hairy and gray
But the playful jester kept the pussies
        pink and shaved.

This master jester knew how to best entertain a cat
He knew the pussy's ins and outs and just where to pat
To please the purring, pretty pussies, he knew the best tricks
The cats would after reward the jester with miry licks.

"The silly king thinks me, this buffoon, a fool
But it takes a fool to ignore my colossal tool
Behold my guitar as I firmly clench it with my hands
And music comes out of it for all the pussies to dance!

Oh, supreme king, have you not seen? 'Tis best to jest than to rule
Pussies prefer, rather than a foolish king, a kingly fool
For a fool knows how to fool around, in and out, of the jewel
But, you, cruel king only know how to bark commands and drool!

Aha! Another lovely pussy for me to rub,
Jack the Jester is my name, and I don't need a glove!"
So if you have a pussy that you would like for Jack to care
Simply lay your pussy in his bed and wait over there.

Sure enough, he will come
As certain as his name is John.

Quotes for the Soul

Proverbs 10: 2 (KJV)

"Hatred stirreth up strifes:
But love covereth all sins."

"No lloro por el amor perdido sino por aquel que no lo ha valorado. No lloro por el amor despreciado sino por aquel que no sabe lo que es ser amado. No lloro por el amor engañado sino por aquel que nunca ha amado. No lloro por el Amor que no fue sino por aquel amor que siendo ya no lo es.

I do not cry for lost love but rather for the one who does not value it. I do not cry for scorned love but for the one who does not know what it is to be loved. I do not cry for deceived love but for the one who has never loved. I do not cry for love that was but for that love that being is no longer so."

Aura Cisneros

Biography

Jafet Reyes-Cisneros is a Hispanic-American poet from Guaynabo, Puerto Rico and Tampa, Florida. He cherishes writing poetry on various subjects, though romance, regret, solitude, parenthood, melancholy, and memory are motifs in his poems. His poems consist of odes, contemplations, narrations and advice. His forthcoming poetry collection, titled "Love Her, Love Her", will be published later in 2022.

He believes that, besides love, the act of artistic creation is the closest humankind can reach toward understanding God the Light Being.

He graduated from the University of Florida with a Master of Science in Aerospace Engineering. He thinks that anime will become the dominant artistic trend, following the past legacies of Westerns and superheroes, and overtake pop culture. If you see him in a bookstore, he will probably be in the manga and comics section.

Published Works

Beneath the Shadow
of the Almond Tree

Upcoming Works

Love Her, Love Her:
A Poetry Collection

Shadow and Shade:
A Novel

From Me to You:
Advice for Life and Hard Times

Harry Barry the Bear

Made in the USA
Middletown, DE
05 May 2022

65255580R00044